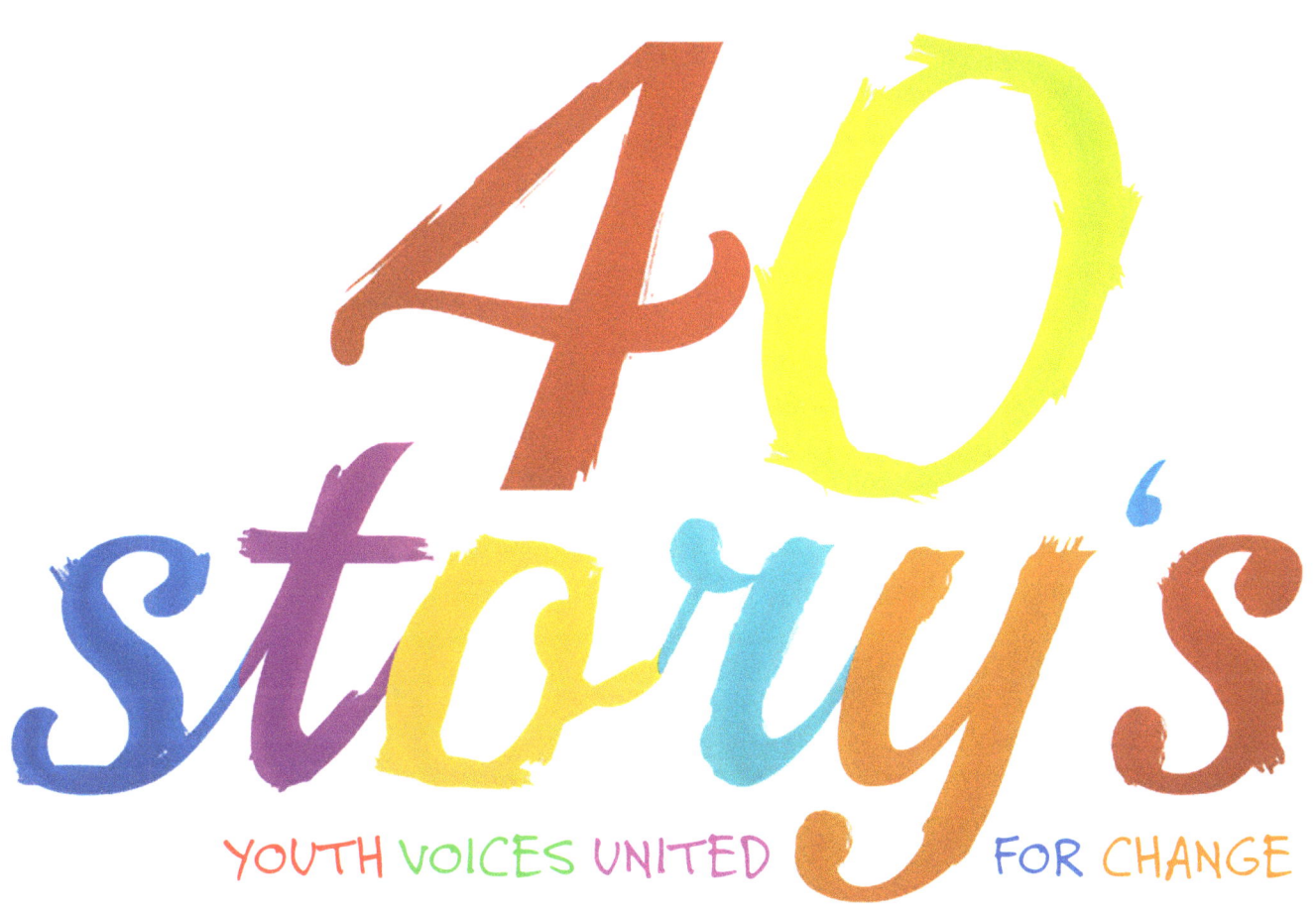

40 story's
YOUTH VOICES UNITED FOR CHANGE

by Creative Children for Charity (3C)

Why 40 Story's?

Now, after taking just one look at the cover, you probably couldn't help but ask one simple question: Why is the title misspelled? Isn't it supposed to be Stories, not Story's? Actually, yes it is! But we misspelled it for so many reasons.

It all started on a cold Sunday morning. The members of 3C gathered together for our usual weekly meeting. We seated ourselves comfortably on the soft, beige couch, and prepared for a productive meeting. The main topic of the day was coming up with a catchy title and designing an awesome logo for this project.

After a long time debating and introducing new ideas, we finally came up with one that not only caught the reader's eye, but also made it unique and stand out. By misspelling the word "stories", and writing it as "Story's" instead, people would naturally feel intrigued and, much like you, dear reader, ask why. The title doesn't only catch the reader's attention, it's also a memorable "mistake" that people are not likely to quickly forget.

It was perfect, and the word some may call a "typo" soon transformed into a unique and special touch that stayed in the mind of any reader who would come across it. By changing the conventional spelling of the word, we hoped to show that youth should not be judged by how they appear on the outside, but by the content of their character. It really all comes down to the saying "Don't judge a book by its cover."

Youth are often seen as no more than kids, who can't hold responsibilities and are constantly creating trouble. But what you see on the outside, is often misleading. Youth are very fun and engaging, and we have the power to become leaders. When we show our true colors, we can make a big difference in our communities.

From the bright engaging colors, to the thought provoking stories that lie on each page, 40 Story's is really the heart and soul of our group's attempt to bring the community together. Inspiring others is the goal of writing this book, and if that goal is met then all of the back breaking hours spent on it would have been well worth it. The time spent getting to know all of the participants and collaborating on this project was exhilarating, and we're optimistic about the book's ability to influence a generation.

40 Story's isn't a typo, it has been created to prove that youth can be youth and still make a difference. Remember, don't judge a book by its cover.

Endorsements

"Encouraging children to charity in this day of digital everything is a necessary and noble effort. These "story's" of real kids and real feelings will resonate with real people."

~Mike Peters, Pulitzer Prize-winning Cartoonist, Dayton Daily News/Creator and Marian Peters,
Antioch Univ. & Int'l Museum of Cartoon Art

"What great lessons for young people…and elders as well. This amazing book written by young adults contains words for ALL of us to live by and "story's" that bring to life these lessons. An absolutely delightful read that should be shared with family and community."

~ Marty Evans, Former Pres., Amer. Red Cross/ Pres.,
LPGA/Exec. Dir., Girl Scouts USA/Sup't US Naval Postgrad. School

"Inspiring and thought provoking ideas by today's youth. 40 Story's is a must read for every youth - young leaders and aspiring young leaders - to understand core leadership assets to help them become caring and responsible citizen of today!"

~ Albert Mensah, Best-Selling Author and Speaker

"40 Story's is a brilliant and inspirational book that reveals the creativity in youth."

~Michael Tetteh, former Seattle Sounder and author of Giftocracy

Copyrights Page

Copyright © 2014 by Creative Children for Charity (3C)

In accordance with the U.S. Copyright Act of 1976, the scanning, uploading, and electronic sharing of any part of this book without the permission of the publisher constitutes unlawful piracy and theft of the author's intellectual property. If you would like to use material from the book (other than for review purposes), prior written permission must be obtained by contacting the publisher at support@MadeForSuccess.net Thank you for your support of the author's rights.

Made For Success Publishing

P.O. Box 1775, Issaquah WA 98027

Visit our website at www.MadeForSuccessPublishing.com

Library of Congress Cataloging-in-Publication Data

Creative Children for Charity (3C)

    40 Story's: Youth Voices United for Change

    p. cm.

ISBN: 978-1-61339-741-1

LCCN: 2014918722

1. Self-Help / Personal Growth / Success
2. Self-Help / Motivational & Inspriational
3. Family & Relationships / General

Book Designed by DeeDee Heathman

Contents

DEDICATION	V
DEDICATION TO PARENTS	VI
ABOUT	
The Team	VII
Creative Children for Charity (3C)	IX
The 40 Developmental Assets	X
SUPPORT	**1**
Family Support	2
Positive Family Connections	4
Other Adult Relationships	6
Caring Neighbourhood	8
Caring School Climate	10
Parent Involvement in Schooling	12
EMPOWERMENT	**15**
Community Values Youth	16
Youth as Resources	18
Service to Others	20
Safety	22
BOUNDARIES AND EXPECTATION	**25**
Family Boundaries	26
School Boundaries	28
Neighborhood Boundaries	30
Adult Role Models	32
Positive Peer Influence	34
High Expectations	36

Contents

CONSTRUCTIVE USE OF TIME — 39
- Creative Activities — 40
- Youth Programs — 42
- Religious Community — 44
- Time At Home — 46

COMMITMENT TO LEARNING — 49
- Achievement Motivation — 50
- School Engagement — 52
- Homework — 54
- Bonding to School — 56
- Reading For Pleasure — 58

POSITIVE VALUES — 61
- Caring — 62
- Equality and Social Justice — 64
- Integrity — 66
- Honesty — 68
- Responsibility — 70
- Restraint — 72

SOCIAL COMPETENCE — 75
- Planning and Decision Making — 76
- Interpersonal Competence — 78
- Cultural Competence — 80
- Resistance Skills — 82
- Peaceful Conflict Resolution — 84

POSITIVE IDENTITY — 87
- Personal Power — 88
- Self Esteem — 90
- Sense of Purpose — 92
- Positive View of Personal Future — 94

MEGA EVENT HIGHLIGHTS — 96

Dedication

This book is dedicated to youth around the world who are trying to figure out their role on this planet. Sometimes life gets tough, and everyone struggles with an identity crisis at a point in their youth. Trying to find our place in society is a challenge, but the most important thing is to be caring and responsible citizens, whether or not we lead conventional lives. Sometimes, as youth, we feel small compared to the world around us, and it doesn't take much for us to feel that way. But what the community doesn't realize is that as youth, we see the world completely different... and we believe we have the power to change the world in our own unique ways to make the world a better place.

Everyone dreams of becoming famous, about being the type of person where everyone knows your name. As youth citizens, we know it feels hard to make a lasting impression on the whole world. We can make a huge difference just on a smaller scale, like in our neighborhoods and schools. And we can do that by acquiring skills and traits, like honesty, integrity, and many more. Being a leader is about having the will and persistence to work towards making a change. The 40 Story's book is written by 60+ youth from their perspective, to help youth around the world explore their core leadership skills and strive to be healthy, caring, and responsible citizens. The 40 Story's experience teaches us to be a reliable citizen no matter where we are, showing a genuine willingness to help others resolve their problems.

We believe today's youth have the power to change the world. And if you look closely, it doesn't always take huge events like 40 Story's to acknowledge that power and see it in action. As youth in the community, we can influence society and the way it functions. So to all those who are reading this, who are trying to find their identity, who feel small compared to the world around them and don't feel like they can make that world, we hope this book provides you with the courage and ideas to become a caring and responsible citizen.

You are important.

As youth we can do great things, every day we help make our community a better place. We may not have changed the entire world yet, but we can make an incredible impact on a number people. We are making this world a better place, one step at a time.

About the Team

Chirag Vedullapalli is 13 years of age and a 8th grader at Chief Kanim Middle School. He is a very talented artist and creates gorgeous art using lots of different mediums including oils and acrylics on canvas. He is a social entrepreneur and supports charities through the sale of his art. He has donated over $20,000 from these sales to many charities including Seattle Children's Hospital, Make-A-Wish Foundation, and others.

Chirag is also the founder of Creative Children for Charity (3C) whose mission is to empower one million kids and teens to donate their time and talent for charitable and social causes. He has spoken at TEDxRedmond and SAM KID 2014. Thus far he has organized over 10 events in various communities and brought thousands of kids and teens to contribute their time and talent to various charities in the region.

In addition to being a social entrepreneur, Chirag is a representative of his school representing over 750 classmates in his school and an active Leo Club member making a difference in the community. Currently he serves as the President for a growing Toastmaster Club. Chirag has won several awards including, Youth Spirit and Trevor Award for community service.

Catalina Raggi, leads PR and Marketing for 40 Story's. Born in Argentina, she moved to the United States when she was two, but considers English her best language. She is 15 years old, and a junior at STEM high school. She has recently won first place at a regional speaking contest.

She is a published poet, and a previous President of a local Toastmasters Youth Club. She has been speaking for almost two years, and although she used to be painfully shy, now loves it. She is also an avid environmentalist who wants to inspire people to care for our planet. Cat often spends her time outside reading, and loves it whenever it is sunny, something which can be rather rare in Seattle.

Also, Cat is a strong believer in the power of art, and is an officer in her school's National Art Honor Society. She is very grateful to be able to help bring the community together, and is especially thankful to be able to do it in a creative way.

Rohini Mettu leads Partnerships for 40 Story's. She is 14 years old and is a 9th grader attending Skyline High School. She is a very passionate artist, and loves to use her imagination, whether it is through her paintings, her music, or her writing.

Rohini is also a snowboarder and martial artist. She is only two belts away from black belt, a journey that has taken her almost 5 years! She is very grateful for her martial arts training, because it has affected her in many positive ways. She finds it to be a very good way for her to relieve stress and clear her mind of worries. She has made many good friends, and is a much stronger person now, both physically and mentally. It has transformed her from a very introverted, shy girl to an outgoing and confident teenager.

In addition to this, Rohini is a very strong supporter of the LGBT community and their rights. She believes that all people are born equal and have the right to choose how they live their lives without nearly as many restrictions. She is very happy to be a part of 3C, and very proud of the positive effect that 3C has on youth in her community.

Dedication to Parents

This book is dedicated to all our parents, for their dedication, kindness, devotion, and selflessness. Thank you for your support, and for all the time you put in to help us grow and become caring and responsible citizens, and leaders in our community. This poem is dedicated to our amazing parents, written by Moira O'Shields.

And I Love You So,
The beauty of your eyes,
The kindness of your actions,
The value of your heart,
And I love you so,

The kisses before bed,
The twirl of your blue dress,
The garden of your hand,
And I love you so,

The times you've saved the day,
The pillar of your strength,
The power of your wisdom,
And I love you so,

The hope in your smile,
The twinkle in your eyes,
The memories with you,
 And I love you so,
 And I never let go

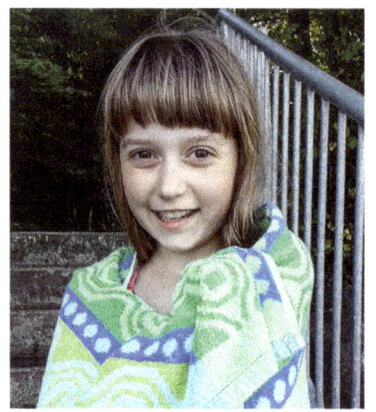

Moira O'Shields is 11 years old. Moira is active in school and was the Master of Ceremony for the Martin Luther King assembly at her school. She plays flute, sings in recitals every year, loves to swim and her favorite past time is to read and draw.

About Creative Children for Charity (3C)

Creative Children For Charity (3C) is a program that supports non profit mission by bringing kids and youth together through art and leadership programs in the community. The mission? To inspire one million kids and teens to donate their time and talent for a social cause. The group strives to unify the community by bringing art together with charity and help those in need. 3C believe in the abilities of today's youths, and want to empower them to donate their time and creativity to a good cause. Fundraising events are regularly done, from which all of the profits go to various charities. One of 3C's main goals is to try to promote the young artists of today, and the creativity which is such a fundamental part of leadership.

3C started with one person, Chirag Vedullapalli, who painted and sold paintings since he was young with support from his family, friends, and the community. At nine, he realized that the talents of others could also be used to help those in need, and 3C was founded.

The group started small, with only three kids showing incredible initiative by organizing events to fulfill the mission, and slowly began to grow.

Along with the events, 3C has also run workshops that generally run for a few hours and focus on a theme. During the workshops, kids are given instructions on creating their masterpieces.

Currently, 3C has raised and donated over $10,000 in last 3 years for the various organizations it's worked with, and over 700 hundred kids participate in our events. The latest project 3C is working on is called 40 Story's, and focuses on strengthening leadership qualities in the youth involved.

Visit http://meylah.com/3c for more information

About the 40 Developmental Assets

The 40 Developmental Assets were founded in 1990 by the Search Institute, which released a framework that identified a set of skills, behaviors, and relationships that enable youths to develop into mature adults and leaders. Over the following two decades, the development assets helped kids through school programs and were widely utilized in the world. William Damon from Stanford University described these assets as a "sea of change" in adolescent development.

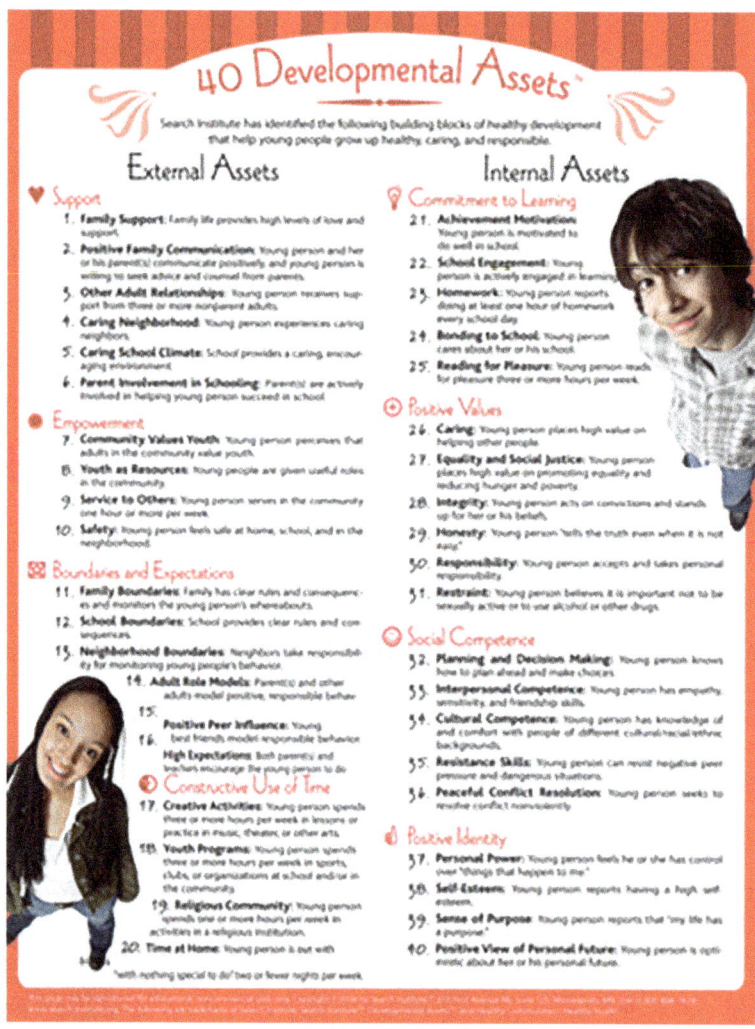

Search Institute has identified the following building blocks of healthy development, known as Developmental Assets, which help young children grow up into healthy, caring, and responsible citizens.

Support

Family Support

Our Family Love — Family will always be there to help when you need them.

Ryan and Tristan Alexander

Ryan and Tristan are two brothers who enjoy Minecraft and building LEGOs. Both love to play games and hang out with friends. They train in Tae Kwon Do and enjoy raising money, collecting goods and other items for those in need.

Ricky is a five-year-old boy who loves riding his bike. He always likes to ride around the neighborhood with his older brother and his family.

There's one problem, he has training wheels. He feels this is a problem because all his friends and family have two wheels. As a result they ride way faster than him. So Ricky decides to change this by learning to ride with just two wheels! It is hard at first. His dad took off the wheels and Ricky could barely balance on the bike, let alone ride it! He fell down often and got many scrapes and bruises. His mom was very supportive and helpful, and cleaned and put a Band-Aid on his cuts.

His older brother, Kian, was his main teacher. He showed him how to easily balance and get on and off the bike. Kian would hold the back of the bike seat and help Ricky balance as he rode the bike. One day he was doing that and Ricky went really fast and started going really far. He looked back at Kian. Instead of being right behind him Kian was really far away. Ricky soon realized that he rode all that distance by himself!

After doing a few rounds around the block he ran into the house screaming, "MOM! DAD! I did it!" His family was so proud of him and Ricky was so thankful that they supported him through this fun experience.

Positive Family Communication

What Family Means

The power of family is that they come together when you need them the most!

Sonali Joshi

Sonali is a 14 year old who loves to draw, do karate, and be outside (not be stuck in a building all day!).

Sophie is a chipmunk who has a family just like you and I. She lives with her mom Cindy, her dad Joe, her two brothers Jack and Shawn. Sophie was very different from her siblings. She often daydreamed and talked to herself. She was also the smallest one in her family so she was made fun of by her brothers. Sophie was also very clumsy and hurt herself a lot, but her siblings would never care to ask if she was okay. That was how her family usually was... her brothers never really talked to her.

One day Sophie's mom told her siblings to go look for acorns and Sophie followed along to help. Her brothers never followed directions and instead of gathering acorns they started throwing them at each other. Sophie wanted this to be her chance to prove something to her family, that even though she was small she could still get work done. Sophie began searching for the perfect acorn to bring back to her parents.

Finally she spotted it on a branch of the tallest tree in the forest. Her parents forbade her from climbing it because she could seriously injure herself. Sophie looked back to make sure her siblings were not watching and continued. She had reached the tip of the branch and the acorn was within her arms reach when she heard a cracking noise. She thought this was the end. What she didn't know was that Jack and Shawn had heard the cracking noise and rushed over to the tree.

The branch broke and Sophie started falling. Seconds before she was going to crash into the ground Jack caught her. Her brothers brought her back home. They explained to their parents what had happened. No one was upset. She thought that her siblings would never care if she was in danger but she was wrong. It was then that she realized that no matter what happened her brothers would always be there for her. She realized the value of family.

Adult Relationships

Adult to Others

Positive relationships with adults can inspire children to become better people.

Morgan Pettersson

Morgan loves design and has been doing art ever since she was a little girl.

"Sweet Dreams, Nora." Nora's nanny, Lilly, kissed her on the head, shut the light off, and left Nora's room. Lilly was like Nora's mom, and really loved her. Nora's parents were always going on business trips, so Lilly took care of her while they were gone.

Nora thought of all the things Lilly would do for her. She would make her breakfast, lunch and dinner, drive her to school, and help her with homework. She would kiss her every night when she went to sleep, and give her a big hug when she came home from school.

That night, Nora decided that she wanted to be just as smart, caring, and loving as Lilly was. She then fell into a deep sleep, waiting for Lilly to wake her up the next day.

"Wake up, Nora! Today is Saturday!" Lilly said. Nora was excited. Saturdays were the days her and Lilly spent the whole day together. Lilly made her a heart shaped bagel for breakfast, and soon they both went out. They went to the park, and Nora saw a homeless man waiting at the entrance. Lilly always gave homeless people money, so Nora put three dollars into his hat.

Nora smiled at Lilly and the two continued walking. They played lots of games in the park like tag, catch, and Frisbee. They got really tired so Lilly and Nora decided to walk down to the fountain and rest there. When they got to the fountain Lilly handed her a brown paper sack. Inside was Nora's lunch: A peanut butter and jelly sandwich, a bag of almonds, an apple, and for desert she packed homemade cookies!

As they sat on the edge of the fountain eating their lunch, Lilly turned towards Nora. "I am very proud of you for giving three dollars of your own money to that homeless man by the entrance!" she said. "I did it because I've seen you do it so many times, and I want to be just like you!" Nora replied.

Lilly then gave Nora a really big hug. She couldn't wait for next Saturday.

Caring Neighborhood

To Help Someone in Need

A good neighbor is the best thing that can happen to all of us. Be engaged in your neighborhood and help your neighbors whenever you can.

Isha Kshirsagar

Isha is a 13 year old going into freshman year. Her hobbies and passions include dancing, swimming, painting, reading, writing, traveling, and hanging out with her friends.

Horror struck through Alia's mind. It was cancer, the doctors had confirmed it. Her mother had been in the hospital for three weeks now, and so had Alia. She had gotten barely any sleep for three weeks and she was feeling tired, hungry, and very stressed out.

Suddenly, two shadows appeared behind the white screen door. Just as Alia began wondering who it could possibly be, the door opened. An old couple walked through the door, bringing food and some clothes with them. They were her neighbors, and very close friends to her mother.

"We came to give you our comforts. We brought you some snacks, Alia, a change of clothes that were lying around in our house, and some other things that would come in use."

Alia couldn't be any more thankful than she already was, until the old lady pulled out an envelope from her purse. "On behalf of the whole neighborhood, my husband and I held a garage sale to raise money for you and your mom. Go on now, take it dear, it is all for you. We're also open to help you with anything you need, Alia, and you are welcome to stay with us anytime you want too."

And for the next few weeks, Alia couldn't get enough "thank yous" to everybody who helped her. The neighbors came by every two or three days to check up on her mother. Soon, Alia's mother was moving quickly on the road to recovery, and the two were finally able to come back home.

They were surprised to see their house fully cleaned, and food left in the fridge for them to eat. The neighbors often came by to help Alia and her mother with daily household chores. Alia was more than grateful for all the support she had been getting these past few weeks, and she didn't know what she would do without all her caring neighbors.

Caring School Climate

Helping Hands are Happy Hands

An accepting school environment gives support to all students, no matter their differences.

Andrea Tang

Andrea takes art in school and likes to help out at camps or at small booths. She also likes to listen to music and do artistic things. Her favorite sports are rock climbing and track. Her favorite colors are orange and purple.

Before stepping out the door something caught Josh's eye. His old skateboard was leaning against the bookshelf. He missed skateboarding but unfortunately he had recently met with an accident at a skateboarding competition. Now Josh was temporarily stuck in a wheelchair but he decided that nothing would get in his way. However, he didn't expect his biggest challenge to be fitting through the school door.

When Josh's school was built, the builders didn't think a person with disabilities might go to this school. He didn't find himself much different compared to other people other than that he sat in a bulky wheelchair. Otherwise he was always treated the same by family members and friends.

The school created a ramp just for him, so that he didn't have to go around the school and go through the back door. They built bigger doors for people of all sizes and shapes. People would open doors for each other and help Josh reach for things that were too high. Yet he still had his independence. He would hang out with his friends at the lunch table and use the same materials as any other kid. He still had gym class and attended assemblies even though he would occasionally arrive late due to the fact that he had to use the elevator to get to the gym.

Josh loved middle school and appreciated that no one treated him any differently than others. It inspired him to help other kids with disabilities. Occasionally he would need help too, but only with small things. Schools lend helping hands to all students no matter how different they are because as long as they are helping, they are happy.

Parent Involvement in Schooling

Volunteer Day | When parents are involved in their kids' lives, children are able to learn better.

Emma Reishman

Emma is an 11 year old who loves soccer, basketball, gymnastics, and acting. She considers herself a very funny and nice person.

Amy O'Hara sits in her second grade classroom, staring up at the clock. It was 1:30, which meant it was time for science! Amy's class was learning all about the ocean.

The teacher came up to the front of the room and announced to everyone, "Okay kids, today is a very special day. We get to learn about underwater fossils! We even have some real fossils here with us in the classroom today. Because these are very fragile, I need you all to be extra careful. Also, we have a special guest who is here to help us, Amy's mom, Mrs. O'Hara!" Amy gasped in surprise.

She didn't know her mom was volunteering in class today! The class divided into groups that went into different stations, where they learned what a fossil is and how it is made. Amy went from station to station, filling out her worksheet eagerly. She did all the drawings, finished writing the definitions, and completed the matching parts. But when she got to the fill-in-the-blank portion of the worksheet, Amy had no idea what to do!

Her mom could see Amy's confusion, so she came over and said, "Amy, it looks like you could use some help." Amy nodded her head, and for the next few minutes Amy and her mom sat and worked on finishing the fossils worksheet. By the end of class they had finished the worksheet, and Amy was really grateful that her mom was involved with her school and learning, so that she could help Amy learn more.

Empowerment

Community Values Youth

Looking Out the Window

Always help people in your community with acts of kindness.

Kushi Lam

Kushi is in the Student Council of her school. She loves to help people out and her hobbies are drawing and dancing. She considers herself shy but the more she knows someone, the less shy she is. Even when she's shy, she is a people's person. She has been dancing since she was 2 and drawing since she was 3.

It was a cold winter morning. Ms. Tammy looked outside the window at the puffy white snow, which fell the previous night. Ms. Tammy had recently graduated from college last summer and was now a first grade school teacher. She was very tall and had long, wavy brown hair.

She was drying her hair by the window while waiting for her grandmother, who she had invited for a short stay during the winter break. She wondered if her grandmothers' flight might have been delayed due to winter snow. Suddenly she saw a cab drop her grandmother off across the street. She wanted to go and help her grandmother cross the street because the road was very slippery due to snow.

Before she stepped out, she saw one of her students talking to her grandmother. His name was James; he was little and full of energy. Then James started walking Ms. Tammy's grandmother across the street. Ms. Tammy was nervous because James was young and hasty. Finally they crossed the street and start walking towards the front porch. Ms. Tammy was now watching them walk on the glistening grass. Once they reached the front door, Ms. Tammy felt very relaxed that her grandmother had reached home safely.

Ding, dong! Ms. Tammy heard the bell ring as she rushed towards the door. When she opened the door, her grandmother gave her a big hug. Ms. Tammy thanked James for helping her grandmother cross the road and bringing her safely to the front door. She gave him a candy bar as a token of appreciation. James told Ms. Tammy a few things he did during the winter break and then he left.

Then her grandmother told her how sweet James was. She told her that James first kindly asked her who she was and if he could help her walk across the street. On the way home he also asked her how she is doing and where she is from. Both Ms. Tammy and her grandmother had a great winter break together. From that point onwards, Ms. Tammy valued James more because he was helpful in the neighborhood.

Youth as Resources

Chief Seattle — Youth should have respect for culture and traditions.

Serenity Schester

Serenity is 13 years old. Her favorite city is Seattle because of the inspiring art that the city has. Her favorite art sculptures are the totems.

CRACKLE! CRUNCH!

The dry leaves crumbled under Ahoti's brown, leather shoes. The cold Seattle air bit his skin, and with each breath a foggy cloud was released into the air. Ahoti had just finished his work at the market, when he got home he decided to show his son, Loki, a place that was very special to him.

Ahoti was a Native American, and though his family didn't live in a tipi or hunt fish or wear feather headdresses, he always had a deep respect for his ancestors, along with their cultures and traditions. His great grandparents were actually part of Chief Seattle's tribe many years ago, and through stories told by his parents and grandparents, Ahoti came to realize how much their land had changed. He explained to his son that what once was a small forest was now a large apartment complex. What once was a river to catch fish in was now a covered by a dark grey road.

He explained that where there is bad, there is good as well. While the beaver population had been greatly damaged because of Native American hunting, local environmentalists helped their number increase once again. Suddenly, Ahoti and Loki were covered in a big shadow. They looked up, their eyes meeting a familiar sight. In front of them stood a tall totem pole, one that had been there for hundreds of years. It was a reminder to the world about Chief Seattle and his tribe, about Ahoti's ancestors, and the Native American culture.

Ahoti loved coming here, it made him feel like he had gone back in time to when the Native American's lived there. Ahoti told Loki that kids, and the youth of the community, have the power to change the world. They could turn simple objects and places into amazing things. Loki now saw the world differently. He saw things from a new perspective. How he had the power to do great things and make the world a better place.

Service to Others

A Bright World
Helping others give you a sense of purpose and can't be done with a reward in mind.

Delaney Rasumussens

Delaney is in second grade. When she was little, her dad always took her along on nature walks. They went mushroom hunting, berry-picking, and geocaching. She has always loved being outdoors and wants to help our planet stay clean.

BUMP! BUMP! The bus went up and down as it turned into the parking lot of the Sunset Hill Beachside Retirement Village. The sun was shining, the summer air was warm and thick, and the waves of the beach were crashing down onto the soft, smooth sand.

Flynn and his class were there for an end-of-school field trip to help the elderly. While they waited to be called in, the kids watched a marathon going on nearby. Finally, the doors opened. When the eager class got inside the village doors, two men greeted them.

"Hello, my name is Elijah and this is my brother Julian. We own the retirement village along with our parents, Carl and Ellie," said Elijah.

"Today you kids will have a lot of fun jobs that will help the people living here, including escorting them to their rooms, helping in the kitchen, and cleaning the rooms," said Julian.

Everyone got assigned a task, and Flynn's task was to help serve lunch in the cafeteria. He washed his hands, and put on rubber gloves, a hairnet, and an apron. Soon people started pouring in, and Flynn served lots of food to them, from mashed potatoes to carrot juice. When the day was over, everybody was tired, and ready to go home. But before they went home all the kids joined the senior citizens outside by the beach. The sky glowed bright red, orange, and pink. The beach water was a calm, deep blue, and everyone stood on the patio enjoying the beauty of the world around them.

Flynn was calm, and felt satisfied and happy because of what he did that day. Helping others made him feel important, and he realized how important it is for everyone to learn to help others without expecting something in return.

Safety

The Protectors | You have the power to become the protectors of our community!

Neal Vedullapalli and Anikait Vishwanathan

Anikait and Neal both are close to 8 years old. Neal loves technology and cars. Neal is working a HUGS project where we wants to inspire the kids and parents to hug more! Anikait will be starting third grade. He loves science and technology, playing video games and LEGO. Destination Imagination, LEGO and video games help him to be creative, innovate and experiment without limits. In addition, he loves martial arts and playing the violin.

Once upon a time in the city of Seattle, there were many buildings getting robbed. There was a beautiful red brick building, which used to get robbed all the time. There were four people who lived in that building, Sam, Julie, Alexandra and Martin. Sam was a car designer who used to create cool cars. Julie was a dancer who used to travel around the world to do performances. Alexandra was a chef who made Italian food in a local restaurant. And Martin was a photographer who often forgot to close the doors of the building when he went out.

All the four people would never talk to each other because they did not have time to meet. The robbers knew about this and took advantage of it. All the four people got robbed lots of times and they were losing lots of money.

One day Sam saw Martin in the hallway and they discussed the problem. Then they met with Julie and Alexandra. They all decided to solve this problem together, but they could not do it by themselves. They needed an expert. They had heard about a scientist named Robert who was a genius in creating a shield for the buildings. Even if Martin forgot to lock the building, the shield would not allow anyone who did not live in the building to come in. They met with Robert.

He installed the shield when everyone was gone. This shield was installed outside the building. The robbers could not believe that the owners of the building put up a shield! They decided to try to and break it. They came, checked and touched the shield....BOOM! BOOM! The robbers were electrocuted, and thrown backwards, and the shield protected the building.

From then onwards, there was no robbery in the building. What Sam, Martin, Julie, and Alexandra realized is that when you talk to people and work together to find solutions, you become the protectors of your community!

Boundaries and Expectations

Family Boundaries

Mason Time-Out

Family boundaries need to be respected in order to keep a peaceful environment.

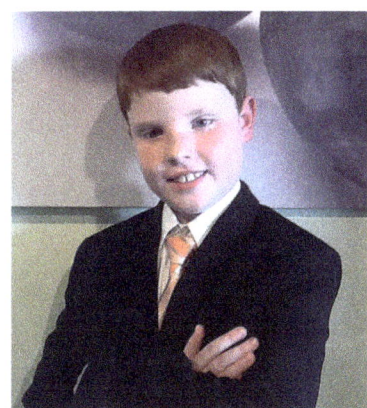

Preston Matthews

Preston is nine years old. He is in the third grade and is the oldest of four siblings. He loves technology as well as playing with friends outside.

"Please stop poking me!!!" screamed Mason's little brother, Max. But Mason ignored him and continued to laugh at Max and poke him. But a few seconds later Mason's mom came home, barely walking through the door when Max sprinted to her, crying and telling her about how his brother was rudely poking him and wouldn't stop.

Mason's mom, who was already tired from work, scolded Mason for being mean to his brother and not stopping even when Max asked him nicely. A bad deed like this left Mason's mom no choice but to send him to the dreaded time out corner. Mason tried his best to get out of it. He tried apologizing, crying, and running upstairs, but nothing worked. In a few minutes, Mason found himself sitting in the timeout corner, which was a corner in the garage with nothing but a chair.

After about ten minutes, Mason's mom let him back in. Mason promised not to poke Max for fun anymore, and that he will stop being mean to Max the minute he says stop. Mason's mom explained to Mason that it's important to respect the feelings of your family, and that if you cross the boundaries and rules that the family has set, then there will always be a consequence for it. Mason nodded his head in agreement, and ran off to the backyard with Max and started playing basketball with him. Max finally realized that he needed to respect family boundaries.

School Boundaries

School Rules | School rules are important in order to keep everyone safe.

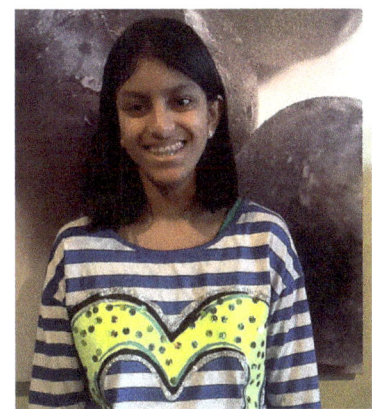

Pankhuri Singhal

Pankhuri is 14 years old and likes to write, listen to music and sing. She is a violinist and plays in her school's orchestra. She is in her chess club as well, and helps the other players meet their standards. Her favorite book genre is fantasy.

"Ok, class, I have to talk to you," said Mr. Spark. The class looked up as one. "Tomorrow...there shall—" He was cut off by an unexpected BEEP! From the loudspeaker, and the principal spoke.

"Good afternoon, kids. Today I have a special announcement to make. Tomorrow we are not going to follow one school boundary called 'no bullying'—"

"WHAT?!" the class whispered loudly.

"—and this is just an experiment to see how well you behave when there is no 'no bullying'. Thank you for your time." The loudspeaker clicked off. Immediately, the class started buzzing excitedly, with many students worrying as well. So Chloe went up and asked Mr. Spark.

"Sir, does it mean that when someone is bullying someone in class, you're not going to stop that person?" asked Chloe.

"I guess we shall find out tomorrow. After all, it's only for a day." replied Mr. Spark.

"Right. It's like we're the citizens of Massachusetts and we won't ratify the Constitution, although this is temporary." Chloe exclaimed.

Mr. Spark smiled, appreciating her knowledge of the US before it became, well, the US. Chloe went back to her seat, wondering why the principal had asked them to see how well this 'rule' would work. Did she actually want half the kids with bruises and bumps by the end of the day tomorrow?

The morning came, and kids suddenly turned from behaved students to bullies. Kids were being tormented even before school started, and it went something like this: a few of them teamed up on one poor kid. Ten seconds later...another gang had beaten up the people who were bullying the person before. And so on and so forth, a chain reaction happened. Everyone in school was bullied by everyone. Ouch. As soon as Chloe walked into the building, someone punched her arm—hard. As Chloe furiously rubbed the spot, Chloe thought, this is the experiment. Great job. Chloe was being jostled and shoved as much as others. Chloe didn't like it at all. That is when Chloe woke up and realized it was nothing but a dream.

Even in the dream, this was for one day, and one boundary, one rule was broken, and everyone, the kids, big and small, the staff, the principal, was not happy. Think about life, and how different it would be without these helpful rules and boundaries.

Neighborhood Boundaries

IT TAKES A VILLAGE

Earth Day | It takes a village to make a difference in your community.

Thomas and Johnathan Szudzik

Johnathon's interests include basketball, drawing and gaming. He has lived in Washington his entire life. Thomas likes to play piano, Minecraft, and take his dog for walks. During these walks he picks up any litter he finds to keep his community clean.

He said he'd be here ten minutes ago! I don't want to be late! Leo thought, wondering where his best friend, Percy, was. After what seemed like forever, Leo heard the heavy knocking of wood followed by three rings of the doorbell. Finally! Leo walked out of his front door wearing his garden gloves, old clothes and dirty sneakers. He was greeted by Percy, wearing a similar outfit. Where were they headed dressed like that? They were headed to a neighborhood gathering to clean up the park across the street, to celebrate Earth Day.

As Percy and Leo got there, they saw all their neighbors had already started to pick weeds, pick up trash, pull trash out of the lake, and clean the park equipment. Percy's next door neighbor, Leslie, walked over to Leo and Percy, handing them two buckets and nets.

"Hi! Our job is to take out any trash from the water." She said. As they headed to the lake, Percy couldn't help but say, "This is amazing! Even the little kids are helping out!" Leslie and Leo agreed, and they started picking out gum wrappers, lollipop sticks, and water bottles from the lake water. Within a few hours, the park looked good as new, and one of the little kids said "Can we do this every year!" It had been such a success that people were more than happy to do it again soon. And so, every year, all the people, kids, and adults, living in that neighborhood would come to clean the park as an Earth Day tradition.

You see, it's not always easy for one person to make a huge difference in their community; it takes a village to create an impact. If everyone comes together, they can get a huge job done, and in the process they shape today's youth in a positive way.

Adult Role Models

Lighting the Path | Adult role models act as an inspiration for the youth of today to grow into the leaders of tomorrow.

Chirag Vedullapalli, Rohini Mettu, and Catalina Raggi

Chirag, Rohini, and Cata are the lead organizers of 40 Stories. The three met at their Toastmasters club and bonded over their passion for youth empowerment and leadership. Chirag is 13 and is a devoted artist. Rohini is 14 and loves to snowboard, paint, and write. Cat is 16 and likes poetry and encouraging environmentally friendly practices.

Every year, the kids of Evercrest High School had a race. Despite being optional, everyone was encouraged to participate, and most kids looked forward to running it. At the end of the finish line, over 3 miles away, the principal stood, holding a lit golden cup.

Out of all of the kids in the school, there was one that was particularly looking forward to the race. Jin Tang was determined that he would be the one to win this year. He wasn't a particularly good runner, but he was certainly spirited, and he was confident that he would win the trophy. Jin trained hard every day to prepare himself for the race. He ran 3 miles a day to make sure he was ready to win. Jim got his inspiration to train so hard, from his elderly neighbor, Mr. Goldman.

Jin met Mr. Goldman when he was playing around the neighborhood a few months ago. With his gnarled cane, Mr. Goldman would spend hours at a time telling Jin stories of his time as a runner when he was Jin's age. As Mr. Goldman and Jin grew closer, Jin wanted to become like Mr. Goldman more and more, and saw running as a way to be closer to him.

When the day of the race finally came, the starting bell rang, and Jin took off along with all of the other runners. Mr. Goldman's inspiring stories flashed through Jin's mind, as he pushed on towards the finish line of the race. Before he knew it, Jin was in first place, and quickly approaching the finish line. Mr. Goldman's old, wrinkled face was beaming with pride, as he cheered Jin on. Jin forced his way through his exhaustion, and ran straight through until the end, taking the flaming cup from his principal's hand.

During his victory speech, Jin made sure to thank Mr. Goldman for all of his encouragement and inspiration as he trained. He knew that Mr. Goldman had been a positive role model for him, and helped him achieve this victory, while making him a better person.

Positive Peer Influence

Stepping Up | The kind actions of one can inspire many others to act as well.

Andrea Zamora

Andrea is nine years old and is in fourth grade. She loves painting, and wants to be a doctor when she is older.

"Okay class, ten minutes until school ends!" Mrs. Ross called. Everyone got up and ran to their backpacks and lined up at the door, leaving the classroom in a huge mess. Papers were everywhere, chairs had fallen over, and pencils lay on the ground. "Kids, can you help me clean up the classroom?" But everyone just ignored Mrs. Ross's voice, excited for summer break to start.

Mrs. Ross kneeled down and began to clean the cluttered classroom. She mumbled complaints about how she was getting late for her flight in the evening. "Mrs. Ross, can we help you with the mess?" said Elisa, Cayla, and Anna.

"Oh yes! Thank you for stepping up and helping me clean up." As Elisa, and Cayla picked up the last papers, Mrs. Ross and Anna put the tables and chairs back in place.

"Thank you for the help girls," said Mrs. Ross. "I hope you three have a great influence on your classmates. Have a great summer."

RIINGGG!!! That was the bell, announcing the end of the school day. "Class, before you leave, please give a round of applause to Cayla, Anna, and Elisa for cleaning up the room," CLAP! CLAP! CLAP! "Goodbye, have a great summer!" But everyone was in action. Everyone began to clean the room!

Mrs. Ross was very happy that these three girls could make such a positive influence on the class of thirty-five. Three kids picking up papers from the ground could lead to thirty-five kids arranging desks, wiping the whiteboard, and arranging the classroom library.

The class realized they all had the power to step up and help others, and in the process, inspire their fellow peers.

High Expectations

The Upward Challenge — Even when the odds are against you, setting a high expectation can help you perform better.

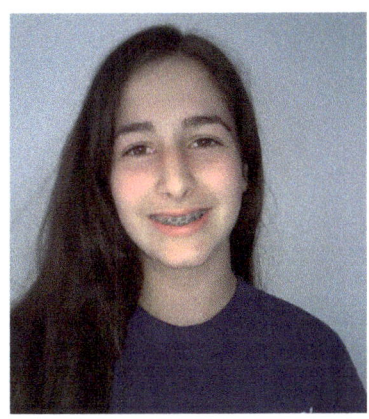

Sydney Otto

Sydney is a freshman. She loves nature and the environment, so she tries to help clean it up on beaches, parks, and roads as much as she can. She especially loves the beach and the water. Her family and she boat and swim a lot, and love to skimboard. The ocean is especially important to her so keep it clean.

Jackie, a 15-year-old freshman, has been awaiting August 10th, because that was the day she would bike in a race for 50 miles. She expected herself to finish the race. With the race happening in the next 24 hours she couldn't wait, it was so hard to get to sleep because she had so much excitement. Eventually, she fell asleep at 1 a.m. in the morning. When she woke up the next day, she was mentally prepared for the marathon, but physically was tired. She realized that by going to sleep at 1 a.m., her body couldn't get enough rest, so she decided to get her adrenaline pumping by going on a quick jog. Ten minutes later, she got back home and she felt so much better than when she had left for the jog.

Jackie's dad, Brad, made an awesome breakfast of sunny side up eggs. Jackie got dressed and couldn't wait to get to the starting point of the event. While they were driving, Brad said to Jackie, "If you are tired, exhale, inhale, exhale, and just keep moving forward no matter how steep the slope is." After hearing this, Jackie had no idea what he was talking about, but before she could put more thought into it, they had arrived at the location of where the event started.

Jackie signed in and arrived at the starting line. In a matter of minutes, the race official fired the gun, and everyone started biking. After biking for 45 miles on mostly flat roads with little hills, finally she had arrived at the last obstacle, Sunset Hill. She could see that the hill would be extremely tough and at the top she saw a little red flag waving vigorously from the wind. She was almost done. As she biked up the hill, she felt her bike going slower, and her legs getting heavier.

Jackie's adrenaline was running out, she was getting tired, she hadn't even gotten the appropriate amount of sleep that night. It took her 30 minutes to bike just 3 miles up the hill, after that she started realizing why the flag was waving so vigorously. It was because the wind was so strong, and sadly it was blowing against her, and this was slowing her down. Just then she remembered what her dad said "If you are tired, exhale, inhale, exhale, and just keep moving forward no matter how steep the slope is."

So Jackie took a few deep breaths and biked at full speed for the last mile. In the last 200 feet, she could see and hear a lot of people applauding for her. She sped to the finish line, and when she biked through the finish line she was informed that she was the fastest in her age category. She realized that setting high expectations actually helped her on her overall performance. Even when the odds are against you, setting a high expectation can help you perform better.

Constructive Use of Time

Creative Activities

Many Masks

Creative activities are a great way to help you express yourself and feel better.

Courtney Huston

Courtney is going into her junior year and is heavily involved with theatre and lacrosse, for which she is goalie. When she acts, she usually specializes in comedy or Shakespeare. She really loves social outreach programs and working with the homeless.

Lyla threw her pencil down in frustration. She had been working on the same math problem for almost twenty minutes, and she still couldn't solve it. She went downstairs to get a drink of water, but was interrupted by the ringing of a doorbell. What day was it? Wednesday. That meant Lyla had theatre class today. She quickly got her stuff together in a bag and left. She carpooled with her neighbor and good friend, Stella. As they pulled up to the church where they practiced, Lyla asked Stella what they were doing today. "I'm not sure," said Stella.

They went to the room with the stage, where their teacher told them that they were doing skits that day. Lyla and Stella got in a group with three of their other friends in the class, and spent the next half an hour coming up with a very funny skit to present to their classmates. Their skit involved lots of hilarious lines, very unique and colorful props, and it was lots of fun to create overall.

They all presented their skit, all the kids laughed, and their teacher said they did a great job. When Lyla came home she was really happy, and because she wasn't in a frustrated mood anymore, she could focus and finish her math homework. She was very happy that she had creative activities like theatre to help her relax and feel better.

Youth Programs

Field Cover Goal | Youth programs allow kids to form bonds with each other and teach themselves valuable skills, including teamwork.

Will Draper

Will Draper is a twelve year old who plays baseball and football. He plays for 3 baseball teams and one football team. He likes to read and spend time outside.

It was the big day. Alfie's chance to help his football team, the Speed Demons, shine. Alfie was the wide receiver, and he had been training for 3 hours every day for this day. Today was the day that the Speed Demons played against the Panthers for the state finals.

As the Speed Demons entered the arena, Alfie could already feel his palms getting sweaty with anxiety. The Panthers had won the finals four years in a row! Almost 300 people cheered them on in the huge bleachers. Alfie was ready. The coin was tossed, and the Speed Demons started with possession of the ball. Alfie was ready for kick off. Once Alfie caught it, his instincts took over for the rest of the game.

Alfie ran past the first line of defenders, but was tackled at the 40. 1st down. Their quarterback throws it down the field but Jonny, their other wide receiver, couldn't catch it. 2nd down.

A short pass to Sean, the team's tight end, and they were able to get to the 55, with 45 more yards to go. 3rd Down.

The ball is passed to Alfie, but the ball was knocked out of his hands. FUMBLE!! Alfie threw himself to the ground to get the ball but Alfie saw Panther jerseys close to the touchdown zone. Alfie ran as fast as he could but saw the referee signal a touchdown. Afterwards, the Panthers scored their 1 point field goal.

Halftime was over, and it was time that the two teams got down to business. It was at the beginning of the 4th quarter when the score was 7-0, then the Speed Demons scored a touchdown. The crowd applauded and cheered. The Speed Demons decided to go for a 2 point conversion so they could take the lead. "HIKE" the play had started, Alfie ran into the touchdown zone and caught the ball when it was passed to him. The crowd went wild, the Speed Demons had got the lead and the score was 8-7.

At the end of the 4th Quarter, with 30 seconds remaining, the ball was in Panther hands at the 40. The Panthers throw the ball to their receiver and get 30 yards. With now 5 seconds remaining, the Panthers decided to go for an easy field goal kick to take the victory. Everyone lines up, and the center yells "HIKE" and the ball gets kicked towards the field goal.

In this moment, everything seems to be going in slow motion. Alfie jumps and blocks the incoming football, and before anyone can react, the game ends at a score of Speed Demons 8 to Panthers 7. All of Alfie's teammates come running towards him and congratulate him for the awesome block. It was the first time that the Speed Demons had won the state finals. At this moment, Alfie was so proud to be involved with this youth program.

Religious Community

A Race Around the World | Every religion offers great stories to learn from.

Ishan Vig

Ishan helps in the community by keeping school safe as a Safety Patroller. He once helped package food for kids in Africa that don't have anything to eat. His passions are playing soccer, basketball, and football.

Ravi came home from school. He had no homework, so he ran upstairs and brought down one of his favorite books, a collection of stories about the Indian God, Lord Ganesha, Lord of intellect and the higher knowledge. Lord Ganesha was Ravi's favorite, because of his cleverness and intelligence. Ravi flipped through the book, until he came to his favorite story of all time, the great race between Ganesha and his brother, Kartikya.

The two brother were having an argument as to who was the elder of the two. They just couldn't decide, so they went and asked their father, Lord Shiva. Shiva decided that whoever could go around the whole world and come back first to the starting point was the older one. Kartikya flew off at once on his peacock, leaving Ganesha behind. But the wise Ganesha simply walked over to his parents, and walked one circle around them. He then went to his father and asked for the prize of his victory.

His father said, "Oh loving and wise Ganesha! How can I give you the prize; you did not go around the world?"

Ganesha replied, "No, but I have gone around my parents. To me, you are my world." And so, Ganesha won the race and was thereafter acknowledged as the elder of the two brothers.

As Ravi finished reading, he went outside to play with his friends. They played soccer, and while they played Ravi kept in mind the religious story he had just read, and hoped to one day be as witty and clever as Ganesha.

Time At Home

Evening Walk

Use your free time at home with loved ones to do things you enjoy doing.

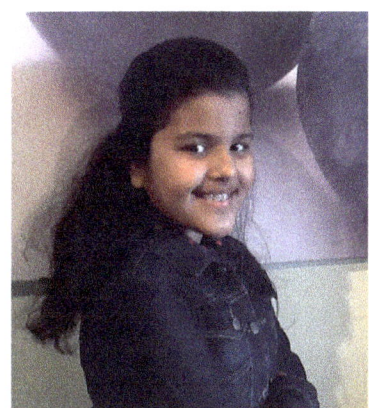

Tanvi Shah

Tanvi loves to read, travel to new places and her passion is art. She doesn't like litter so whenever she sees any at her school or in her neighborhood she picks it up.

Tara checked the time on her clock. 3:00 in the afternoon and she had already finished her homework! When she walked downstairs her mom was surprised she was done already, so she asked her, "You are done already? That was fast!"

Tara replied saying "Well I focused and made sure I did it properly. But now I'm bored, I don't have anything to do!" Her mom suggested they did something fun together. They decided to go and take a walk.

Outside the weather was perfect. The air was warm, there were birds flying everywhere, and it was nice and quiet. As Tara and her mom started to walk, she realized that just being outside made her feel ten times better. While walking they talked about many things, including Tara's school, art, and dance. They walked around her neighborhood, past flower filled gardens, kids riding their bikes, and neighbors walking their dogs. When Tara got back home it was 5:00. She had been outside for almost one and a half hours!

After that, Tara's dad came home so they all played Frisbee outside. After a little bit it started to get dark outside, so Tara and her family went inside, ate dinner and went to bed.

Tara realized that it's important that when you have free time at home, you should spend it with your family, doing things that you like to do. Like taking walks or playing a game.

Commitment to Learning

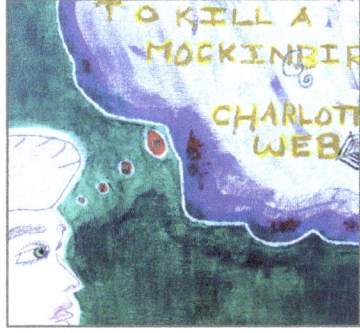

Achievement Motivation

A Hand-y Way to Succeed

When you are motivated to succeed, you'll find yourself making better choices.

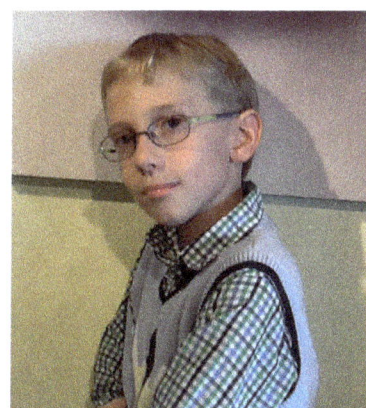

Trey Johnson

Trey is in fourth grade and is nine years old. He loves to do art and believes in helping others do well in school.

Anton and Blake loved school, and more importantly, they loved to learn. Because of this, the two friends always made sure that they were learning as much as possible. They always listened to the teacher and asked questions when they didn't understand something. It wasn't just that they liked their school, everyone at school like them too because they were always kind to everyone, and gave their teachers the respect that they deserved.

One day, Anton and Blake were riding their bikes to school. While riding, they passed by a brand new arcade. The flashing lights and blinking games were too much to resist. Blake stopped and said "What if we skipped school and went to the arcade? Anton was very tempted to go and play, but the local chief of police would be speaking at school that day and he didn't want to miss it.

"Blake, school is important, we can't just skip school because we feel like it! School helps us learn respect and safety. We learn to be responsible, and it helps us so much!" Anton said.

"So what? It's just one day," Blake scoffed.

Anton's determination came flooding back "We need to go to school if we want to learn, Blake! We can't just skip out on the hard work and expect it to not affect us!" At some point during Anton's rant, Blake's enthusiasm had completely deflated, and his dark blue eyes looked down, ashamed. "I guess you're right. I still want to go to the arcade though."

Anton smiled and the two boys decided to have fun at the arcade after school. They realized that because they were motivated to learn, they made the right choices.

School Engagement

Young Mendeleev

Being engaged at school gives you access to a whole new world of knowledge.

Vivek Dutta

Vivek Dutta is thirteen years old and his hobbies include playing soccer and video games. He loves to help his community and believes young people have the potential to change the world.

One day, a young boy named Jack was taking a walk with his father in the woods. As they were strolling through the scenery, the boy suddenly asked his father, "Why are trees green? Why not pink or blue or any other color?"

The father replied back, "Son, that is a great question. The leaves of a tree are filled with a chemical called chlorophyll, which is used by plants to get their food. The sunlight absorbs all colors except green, so our eyes see it as green." Although this was at first incredibly challenging for the young child to grasp, it was a trigger pulled for his curious mind. He was now very interested.

That night, Jack went home and secretly opened up his father's computer to research about plants. Jack began to learn more and more about how plants function and what really makes them look green. His father's answer was indeed correct, but he could now truly understand how it all made sense!

But Jack did not stop there. His research led him to ask many more questions, so he was motivated to continue learning. He spent a lot of time with his chemistry teacher, asking questions and learning about the world of chemistry. He soon realized that he had a great interest and liking towards the study of chemistry.

His passion led him to much success in the future. At school, teachers were flabbergasted with Jack's learning tenacity as he aced every chemistry exam. It wasn't long before one day his father enrolled him in a chemistry camp. Here, Jack could experiment and study different elements, and unlocked secrets he never even thought could be true. Other kids around him learned from him and strived to do the same. Using chemistry as a guideline to taking interest in academics, the fun educational environment and inspirations from elders are what motivated Jack, and soon many others, to go far in life.

Homework

Do Your Homework | Doing your homework helps you memorize all of the new information that you need to know.

Moa Valentin

Moa is in Girl Scouts. She helps the community with her Girl Scouts troop. She likes to sing, play the piano, tennis, dance, and to help her teacher.

"Homework is the equivalent of rain in the summer." Fatima tried to explain to her less than receptive mother as her mom simply stared at her, clearly annoyed. "It's like getting a shot at the doctor office. It's a hot pizza burn on the roof of your mouth! Homework is the exact opposite of everything that Batman stands for!"

At that, Fatima's mother rolled her eyes before stopping her. "Fatima, homework may seem like a horrible thing to you but it is important. It helps you remember and learn all of the necessary things that will help you in school. And by the way, I'm sure that Batman always did his homework."

Fatima sighed and just went back to answering what seemed like page after page of math questions, not so quietly kicking her feet against the table to show her frustration. It was so hard! She had no idea how to answer the questions. The entire concept of fractions seemed too hard to understand. She decided to take a break. Later that day, while baking with her mom, she explained how fractions worked in baking a cake. How you need to use certain fractions and proportions to make the cake sweet, fluffy, and soft. It reminded Fatima of her math homework from earlier that day. Now that she could relate to a real life concept, Fatima felt much more confident in doing her math homework.

When she once again sat down to finish her homework, she found herself relating each fraction problem to her cake baking experience. Having to do her homework helped Fatima cement the information about fractions. It showed her how practicing and understanding her homework could help her do simple everyday tasks. After this, although Fatima still preferred going outside and playing, she now understood that even though it wasn't the most fun task in the world, homework was still important, and that Batman probably did his homework too.

Bonding to School

Eagle's Nest

School can help you expand your horizons.

Helen Li

Helen is twelve years old. She likes to volunteer by planting trees and helping out at special events in the community. In her spare time, she enjoys writing essays, playing piano, and reading. She often goes outside for hikes on trails, too!

"I want to fly like a bird!" Little hands excitedly pumped up and down as Heather looked out the plane window, waving at the eagles flying beside them. She cheerfully told her mother what her future goals were. Her mother laughed. "When you grow up, you will fly like a bird." Heather simply tilted her head, confused by what her mother said, but went off to play with her toys and soon forgot about the words she heard.

As the years passed, young Heather grew. The first day of kindergarten soon came and went, without a single tear from Heather. She soon made friends in her class, and loved her school. In third grade, she gave her first presentation in front of her class, and her teacher praised her for her wonderful performance. Heather looked forward to going to school each day, and cheerfully entered the classroom with a big smile on her face.

One day, many years after she first told her mother about her dream of flying, Heather remembered what her mother told her, and realized that school really had helped her to fly. But not in the way she intended. There, she learned to read, write, do math, and created some of the greatest memories she had. School had helped her achieve her greatest, by making an environment that she loved and in which she felt loved.

In a way, Heather thought, everyone was like a baby eagle, waiting until they were able to leave the nest. It was thanks to school that she was able to spread her wings and see the horizon.

Reading for Pleasure

Don't Judge a Book by Its Cover

Reading books can help you open up doors to new possibilities.

Sophia Ojeda

Sophia is thirteen and is going into eighth grade. She has many hobbies that range from lacrosse, which she is currently playing, and swimming, which she used to do.

Megan is a young girl who is unable to move. Her disability didn't allow her to be independent, so her parents hired an aide for her. Because of this, she was judged a lot, criticized, and bullied. But in reality, Megan is a very kind hearted and smart girl. She learned how to read and write using special tools, because learning was important to her. She absolutely loved reading. Her all-time favorites were "To Kill a Mockingbird" and "Charlotte's Web." The characters in these books always made Megan feel more confident. They gave her hope.

Because of her love for learning, she was enrolled in a gifted program at her school. With the help of her aide, she went through the whole school day without much difficulty. She was quite intelligent, and was soon at the top of her class and she was a favorite of her teacher. That made the other kids jealous, and they felt like her disability was the reason for it.

Some students who were jealous, taunted Megan by making fun of her wheelchair, disabilities, and that she wasn't smart at all. Megan became very angry at these comments, and sometimes was unable to control her body when she got mad.

"What a freak!" They would shriek. These comments made Megan end up having seizures, which made the kids laugh even more. To help Megan calm down, her aide would give Megan her favorite books, and help her turn the pages.

Megan kept reading, and over time, learned to deal with the rude comments and people in the right way. Megan entered many competitions, won awards, and helped her school stand out amongst the others. When she grew up, she told her story in a best-selling autobiography called "Don't Judge a Book by Its Cover".

Positive Values

Caring

Love and Care

Helping other people makes you feel better as well as the people you are helping.

Stephanie Ispas

Stephanie is in her school's Honor Society and does projects to help her community. She enjoys drawing, reading, and is very passionate about getting good grades in school.

It was a hot afternoon. School had just ended, and Claire was walking back home with her friend Gavin. Claire was silent and said nothing the whole way there, because she had a rough day at school. She sighed.

"What's wrong?" Gavin asked.

"Well, everyone's been calling me selfish. So what if I have my own things to care about, like homework, credits for community service, and my projects?" replied Claire.

"I don't think that you're selfish. It's okay to take some time off just taking care of yourself. Hey, since you need credits, why don't you come with me to help out at the local food bank tomorrow after school? You can get community service credits there!" Gavin offered.

"At this point, I'd do anything for credits..." Claire replied

"Yay! Meet up with me in front of the school tomorrow and my mom will drive us to the food bank."

After school, Claire and Gavin went to the local food bank. Gavin showed Claire around and told her the procedure and what she could help with. Claire helped out with organizing the food while Gavin helped out with deliveries. At the end of the day Claire sighed, "I might as well continue to volunteer here. This is a great way for me to get hours for my college resume when I'm older."

After a few days of volunteering at the food bank, Gavin went up to Claire.

"Would like to help me out with the deliveries? Today is especially important because we're donating food to an orphanage that's been running low on money and we want to help out by delivering some food to them." Gavin asked.

"Okay, I'll help." Claire agreed.

When Claire and Gavin arrived at the orphanage, they helped distribute the food. Claire watched the orphans' faces light up with happiness, which made Claire smile too. She turned to Gavin and said, "Helping other people feels amazing! I guess that when you volunteer it isn't the hours for your resume that count, but helping other people, and the happiness that you can give them." Because of their outstanding service at the food bank, Claire and Gavin both received awards from their schools. Everyone realized how kind and caring Claire really was.

Equality and Social Justice

Red | We are all equal, and we should respect each other for who we are.

Vicky Raggi

Vicky is in seventh grade. She is in Toastmaster's gavel club, and likes to volunteer, especially at her local nursing home. She really likes baking as well. She cooks too, but has a very strong sweet tooth.

Ever since Jessica was young, she felt red. However, in her world, people were born colors, and assigned responsibilities. According to her physical appearance, she was blue. Blue people, like her, did all of the cooking and cleaning. Red people were outside, being free. They worked in the fields, and did a lot of the work. Jessica always felt like she belonged with the reds. It wasn't that she wanted their benefits. It was that she had just always felt that she was red. Jessica wanted to be red.

Jessica had never told anyone how she felt about being blue. But one day, on the bus, she told her best friend, Tiffany. When she told her this, Tiffany was silent, and then promised not to tell anyone. They got off the bus, and Jessica felt good. She had finally told Tiffany, and Tiffany had understood. This glee, however, did not last long. By the end of the day, everyone was laughing and teasing her. She wondered how it had gotten out. Surely Tiffany hadn't told anyone. The next day, Jessica found Tiffany in a giggling and whispering group of blues. They all quieted down near Jessica. She turned to Tiffany, searching her eyes for any sort of consolation.

"Um, Tiffany? Where were you on the bus? What happened?" Jessica asked.

"Like I would hang out with a freak like you," Tiffany scoffed. At those words, Jessica stumbled back. "N-no......"

For the rest of the day, Jessica wandered through class after class, hour after hour, silently bearing each insult that pierced her. But after a while, she found that she didn't care. Nothing mattered. Well, except for Tiffany. Tiffany had always been there, no matter what. She always counted on Tiffany to catch her. But now, she wasn't there, and Jessica just kept falling and falling. She bumped into someone, and looked up. Oh god, no. It was Jason. He was perfect. She always adored him, and she couldn't stand hearing his hatred for her.

"Please, just let me go home. Spare me from your hatred and hurtful insults." She pleaded.

"What are you talking about? You are amazing. I really like how you are, and how open you are. I was avoiding you because I didn't think I was worth your time. I-I really like you." He said, shyly.

This was astounding to Jessica. She suddenly felt again. She was accepted. She thought that Tiffany was all that mattered, all that was there to fall back on, but she was being caught by someone else. Someone who accepted her.

"So.... I was wondering.... do you maybe want to hang out sometime? Now that I know that you are red, I could teach you how to work in the fields, and we can be red. Together." Jason asked.

"Yeah, I'd like that. But won't you be teased?" Jessica replied, feeling like she was floating on a cloud.

"I don't care. We are all equal, and if they don't see you for who you are, then I don't want to see them!" Jason joked.

So off they went, together. Ignoring all the whispers and laughs, they were happy, and one day, they found a place where they were accepted, where they belonged.

Integrity

Guarded Beliefs, Alive and Free

Having integrity as a core value gives you determination and fearlessness.

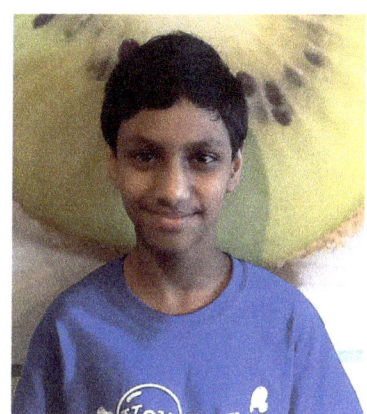

Anirudh Prakash

Anirudh is 13 years old, attends the highly gifted program (PRISM) at his middle school. With his family, he loves to be involved in the book drives, food bank, recycle clothes for a cause. He is in a Future Problem Solver's Club with his school, which teaches him how to be a great citizen of tomorrow today.

"All heed, Moby!" The pod cheered his skilled demonstration of 'breach'. Although depths petrified Moby, he diligently raised higher to repeat his adept flips. Curious to investigate the glimpse of a mysterious white speck, he breached over and over. Tossing things out frantically, a small fisherman struggled to keep his boat afloat.

"Hey! I think that's Vince, he needs help!"

"It is too dangerous, Moby. Vince is a human after all, a foe of marine life," skeptic aunts advised.

"Vince rescued me back to water when I washed up his beach. Now I pay him back, right?" Moby insisted.

"Vince had hundreds of humans to help then," reminded his haughty cousin.

"Our pod is huge, we can help: together," stubborn Moby pleaded his case. "We are no match to angry waves. Whales do not help humans. Forget Vince! Let us move away from storm."

Moby's dad delivered the group verdict. Fight for Vince, or swim to safety: Moby faced his dilemma; his family quickly disappeared.

He chose the neither safe nor popular path. His conscience reminded him about an individual's obligation. Near the shattered boat, Moby's zealous eyes met Vince's terrified pair. He tugged the boat for hours amidst intense squall before reaching the faraway island.

"I wonder where my pod is?" Moby bellowed for family and friends, but the roaring rough waves buried his exhausted call while he drifted in and out of consciousness. When the gale calmed down, a faint light broke out of the sky. Vince patched up his boat enough to venture homewards. He scouted the seas, although, not for fish.

Finally, he found Moby on a large mossy rock, perhaps his shelter! Ecstatic, Vince circled around, waving thanks to his lifesaver. Moby smiled back at Vince, and soon disappeared into the depths. In spite of discouragement from family and friends, he had unwavering principles. He upheld Integrity with courageous willpower to overcome adversity.

Honesty

Being Truthful — Being honest isn't always easy, but it is important to keep relationships strong, and is the mark of a leader.

Hannah Robinson

Hannah is ten years old. She loves to draw, cook, and to design clothes.

Julia and Daphne were best friends since they first met in preschool and now they were in 7th Grade. They were common in almost every way. They both loved the outdoors, shopping, had long hair to their shoulders, and even talked alike. But the only difference was that Julia was very rich as both her parents were CEO's of big companies. Daphne's dad was a garbage man and her mother didn't work, resulting in a lower income. Julia always wore fancy jewelry that she brought from exotic vacations. Daphne was secretly jealous, but didn't want it to get in the way of her friendship with Julia.

One day at school, in gym Julia told Daphne about the diamond necklace around her neck. She said that it was once owned by Queen Elizabeth the First in the 1600s. Daphne felt a sting of jealousy but ignored it. The necklace was beautiful with little pieces of gold threaded through it. The two started their 3-mile run, and Daphne was lagging slightly behind Julia. She saw that Julia's necklace becoming undone, and then that it had fallen to the ground without Julia noticing. Daphne picked it up and started to tell Julia that she had dropped but then looking at it became mesmerized by its beauty. Without realizing it she put in her pocket, and kept running.

Daphne forgot all about the necklace until when at her house Julia called in tears that she had lost her necklace and that she would be grounded for life. Daphne felt ashamed for not telling Julia about her necklace. Crying, she told her dad about everything who told her that it is always better to tell the truth and that Daphne should just be honest to Julia.

The next morning Julia was sulky and miserable and Daphne never got a time to talk to her. The necklace felt heavy in her pocket. She found Julia sitting alone in the corner of the lunchroom.

"Hey Julia, remember the diamond necklace owned by Queen Elizabeth the First?" Julia nodded sadly. "Well, here it is!"

Daphne took the necklace from out of her pocket and handed it to Julia. Julia face brightened just like a sun coming from behind a cloud. "Oh Daphne, you're the best friend I could ever have!"

Daphne looked at her feet and said, "No, I'm not." Daphne then told how she was going to give the necklace but then became greedy and wanted it for herself. She told Julia about what her father had said. "I hope you forgive me, but I won't be angry if you don't."

Julia gave her a big smile and said, "Oh Daphne, you're still the greatest best friend that anyone could have. That's what I love about you. You're always so honest with me. Honesty is one of the traits of a leader and you are a leader."

Responsibility

The World Is In Our Hands

Our World is in Your Hands. Take Responsibility.

Shloak Dutta and Souptik De

Shloak is a 10 year old attending sixth grade. He loves to play soccer, read fictional books and travel with his family. Lionel Messi is his soccer god, Harry Potter his ultimate guru, and Chicago the coolest city on earth.

Souptik is an 11-year-old sixth grader. He likes to cook Italian, Indian, and Mediterranean food, invest in the stock market, play soccer, and hang out with his friends. He likes to stay active and get involved in the world around me.

Everett Jade was an environmentalist genius at the age of 11. He lived in the future when Earth was a blackened place of miserable, dirty, areas. Diseases caused by the oversized garbage dumps killed great numbers at a rapid speed. It was hard to breathe because of the low quantity of plant life. Everett was very disappointed at what his world had become. He lived in one of the worst part of the Earth, where the great population was disappearing thanks to the increasing pollution. Everett figured out that if he didn't change something the human race would die.

Everett called his friends Polina and Spark to help him carry out his new idea. He explained to them that if all three of them could convince the world that by planting trees and plants they would save humanity and countless other species living on earth. Polina, being Everett best friend thought it was a great idea, and Spark liked it too. They started by planting one tree in the middle of their neighborhood. Then they started planting them all over the world. People began to become interested about what was going on. They asked what the three eleven year olds were doing, and they answered, "Saving the world by planting trees. If you want to help, start planting." Soon their community was beautiful and green and all the people kept planting trees and tending for plants.

The three good friends went around the world with other people in their city and convinced more people to help the worthy cause and save the people from extinction. Everyone was now planting and tending. Everett was beginning to accomplish his goal. From there the sky was the limit. The world was turning from black to green again. The three best friends' slogan was Our World is in Your Hands. Take Responsibility. Earth thrived long after the heroics of the three heroes who were honored by being named the Green Three. Their legends will always be in our hearts and we will always remember how they saved the world by going green.

Restraint

BIG DREAMS

Dream Big | Don't give in to peer pressure.

Sara Hansen

Sara is 16 years old. She loves to draw and read in her free time. She is currently in 11th grade. Her favorite class in school is Outdoor Adventures, which is a part of PE. When she's not doing school work, she is doing one of her favorite things, karate. She is also a really big fan of the football season and playing ultimate Frisbee.

Flora was the new girl in town. She didn't have many friends and always felt threatened by the popular kids. Flora was nervous to start out at a new school and lose all her friends, and have to make new friends. She got through the school day, with lots of people introducing themselves, but none of them similar to her old friends. Until one day, Rebecca, a classmate of Flora came up and introduced herself. Flora realized that Rebecca was a lot like her past friends. Rebecca told Flora that she was having a party at a friend's house that night, and Flora was invited. Being a new kid at school without any friends, Flora said yes.

That night, Flora got dressed in her best clothes and waited for Rebecca to pick her up. She was on her way and was really excited. She arrived at the party only to realize that it wasn't like any of the parties she had been to before. There were people who were smoking in the back of the room and people drinking everywhere. It didn't take long before some of them were trying to drawing her in. She had a drink handed to her as soon as they saw there was not one in her hand. She didn't take any because she didn't want to risk having anyone slip something bad into her drink. Soon she met up with Rebecca, who was clearly drunk. Flora was slightly scared, and all she wanted was to get out of there.

She decided that she would leave the party and told Rebecca that she had to go because her mom needed her to come watch her sister. After another five minutes she left the party. Flora was happy that she was able to get away from the party even if it was full of the kids. Flora finally found her perfect group of friends... friends that accepted her and she didn't have to try to be someone that she wasn't.

Social Competence

Planning and Decision Making

Abundance of Ideas

Setting goals and planning helps you achieve your aspirations.

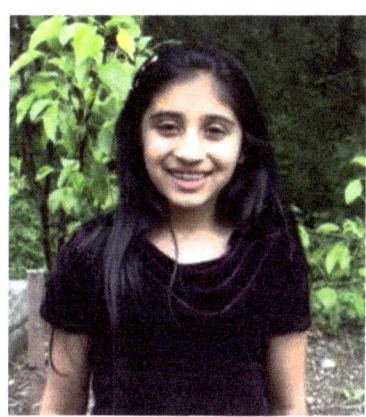

Diya Garg

Diya is a fourth grader and is nine years old. She loves dancing, art, playing the piano, and doing martial arts. She also likes to watch movies and public speaking.

Reyna Greene is an 11 year old, who likes to eat. No, that didn't describe it. She loves to eat. Her meals were usually from fast food restaurants, and were very oily. Every night she would eat a bowl of ice-cream, and she would drink a can of soda after every meal. She loved to watch movies, so she rarely went out and played. She always stayed up late at night watching movies and texting her friends. As a result she never got much sleep. She couldn't do many things, got tired easily, and her health kept getting worse. Her parents tried to convince her to eat more healthy, but she didn't listen. She became obese, and always felt very weak and tired. Then one day at school, Reyna learned that as an end of the year party, her class would be going to a nearby water park. She was very excited about this opportunity, got her parents to sign the slip and then took off for the school bus.

At the park, she went on several roller coasters and hung out with her friends. They went all over the park, from one ride, to the next, to the next. While all her friends were full of energy and excitement the whole time, all the running and playing made Reyna very tired. But she didn't want to make her friends pity her, so she kept running and going on rides. One of the rides involved a lot of spinning, and when Reyna got off the felt very dizzy. All of a sudden her vision was very spotty, and she felt very lightheaded. Before she could make it to the nearest bench, everything went black. Reyna had fainted. When she woke up, the whole class was staring right at her. Her teacher gave her water to drink, and granola bars to eat. She felt embarrassed, and didn't have much fun the rest of the party.

That day when she told her parents everything that had happened she took an oath for the next year; she would eat more fruits and vegetables in her meals. She would take a multivitamin every morning, and limit herself to one hour of TV a day. She would only eat sweets after dinner for dessert, and only drank soda once a week. Reyna also joined a soccer camp, which helped her rebuild her strength and stamina. Within a year, Reyna was once again a very healthy and happy girl. She no longer ran out of breath so easily, and had an amazing year.

Interpersonal Competence

Sunset City | Good friends will always be there to support you.

Megha Jain and Aditi Jain

Megha is in eighth grade and is twelve years old. Some hobbies of hers are painting, drawing, tennis, and basketball. Her favorite subject in school is math.

Aditi enjoys running, art, volleyball, and soccer. She is in sixth grade and eleven years old. She really wants to be either a paleontologist or a marine biologist.

Klaus had spent the whole day running and playing with his friends. He was definitely the kind of person others would think of when they thought of the words "social butterfly". Klaus was nice to everyone, so everyone was nice to Klaus! Because he was so friendly to others, he always had someone who was willing to hang out with him and help him out when he needed it.

That night, the sky was clear and light as sun prepared to make its daily trip below the horizon. The sunset was just a few minutes away, and today, Klaus planned on sitting outside his lawn to watch. He had never really taken the time to look at the sunset before, but realized that it would be an amazing experience. That day seemed like a particularly great choice to watch to sun go down, not only because of the fantastic weather, but because it would be a wonderful way to end an awesome day.

He thought about his friends as the sun slowly began to set, casting purple and pink light over Klaus. A sense of calmness washed over Klaus because he realized that he was never alone because of the big group of friends that he had that were always by his side, supporting him.

And so, sitting on the bright, green grass, Klaus smiled as he watched the beautiful sight of the sun setting, because he knew that no matter what happened, he always had his friends to support him and to help him get through tough times.

Cultural Competence

The Story of OOM | Experiencing other cultures can show you new insights into life.

Teja Sunku and Raj Sunku

Teja is fifteen and going into tenth grade. Raj is ten and going into sixth grade. Raj loves origami and teaches a lot of origami classes in his community

Once upon a time, there was a planet called Oom. Oom was big, very big, five times the size of the earth. On Oom, there was a sentient species called the Oomians. The Oomians were eight feet tall, electric blue creatures. This species was very intelligent and hot tempered. They had four eyes, two in the front and two in the back. The Oomians walked on two legs, could run very fast, and had amazing balance due to their 5-foot tails.

The Oomians fought with each other, sometimes for petty reasons, sometimes for resources that they share among themselves. Over time, the Oomians formed 5 major tribes. Each tribe had its own culture and traditions, each believing that they had nothing in common against the other four except that they all hated each other.

The war grew and the Oomians improved their technology to gain the upper hand. The weapons eventually made the planet unstable, making it likely to explode any second. The Oomians realized that their war was getting them nowhere and instead decided to work together. They split planet Oom into five other planets before it could explode by itself. Today, even though they still argue with each other, they get along much better and people move from tribe to tribe as they wish.

After the planet Oom was split into five smaller planets, they realized the merit of experiencing other cultures, and learned to accept the style and traditions of other religions.

Resistance Skills

The Shining Tree

Resisting negative forces can often result in you becoming a stronger person.

Carlie and Kayla Reese

Carlie and Kayla are fourteen-year-old twins going into their freshman year.

Deep in the woods there was a tree. This tree wasn't like any other tree, it contained all of the vibrancy and color that any tree could. The tree shone brightly in the dark woods where it grew, providing light in the otherwise pitch black forest.

The tree had rested peacefully in the same spot for years. However, dark trees began to grow close to the vibrant tree, threatening to take all of its color and brightness. These trees were jealous of the other tree's individuality and wanted to take that from it and turn it just like the other trees, to turn it dark, and scary.

These trees surrounded the bright tree, creating what seemed like an all-consuming force that left no room for any independence or individuality.

Resisting the negative energy of the older, stronger trees seemed nearly impossible for the poor bright tree, but nevertheless, it desperately fought back. It was very difficult for the tree to fight off the older trees, but in a bright flash of strength, the smaller tree enveloped the older trees in light, causing them to change in form. Their twisted, bare, dark branches became green with leaves and bright with color. They had turned from dark and scary trees to beautiful and vibrant ones.

After this moment, the tree became even more vibrant and bright, and the forest was beautiful. The forest had survived a very terrible situation and been powerful enough to not give in to what the others tried to make it do and become. Thanks to this, the forest would forever hold its lively independence.

Peaceful Conflict and Resolution

Hershey Bar

Listening and understanding each other is a way to resolve conflicts peacefully.

Anna and Lauren Williams

Both Anna and Lauren are chocolate fanatics and love to peacefully resolve their conflicts.

Swish goes the basketball, Dylan had scored 10 out of 10 shots from the 3 point line. Dylan was so proud of himself. Right then, Dylan's little brother Joseph walks into the basketball court and says, "Hi Dylan."

Dylan says "Guess what... I scored 10 out of 10 shots from the 3 point line."

"I don't believe you." says Joseph "Prove It."

Dylan takes one shot, he sadly misses the hoop from the pressure of his brother watching him. The ball bounces of the rim and hits Joseph in the head, and knocks him down.

"OH NO! I'm so sorry Joseph." says Dylan to his 7-year-old brother Joseph after accidentally hitting him with a basketball and knocking him over.

"I can't believe you, you are so evil, I can't believe we are brothers." says Joseph to Dylan in a very mean voice.

"Let me make it up to you Joseph" says Dylan "I'll be right back." he says to Joseph in a sweet voice. Two minutes later, Dylan returns sprinting, holding something behind his back.

"What are you holding." says Joseph.

"A surprise!" replies Dylan.

"PLEASE TELL ME, I really want to know.... please." says Joseph with a cute face. "If you insist." responds Dylan. Dylan then pulls the surprise from behind his back, and he watches his brother's eyes light up as he sees the big Hershey's chocolate bar. Dylan unwraps the chocolate and splits it with his brother.

Joseph says, while gulping down chocolate, "You are the best brother ever, and I'm so happy to have you in my life!"

Positive Identity

Personal Power

Joes Loves Life | Each of us has superpowers we need to use to do right things.

Kesini Sunil

Kesini is in the seventh grade and is twelve years old. She loves to play soccer and spends a lot of time hanging out with friends. She has a younger brother and loves to be outside.

Joe wasn't like normal kids, he had special powers. He had the power to see everyone's emotions, and feel what they felt. He used his power to control the world around him and to make the world a better place. He once went to downtown Seattle and walked by a homeless family on the road. He looked into their emotions, and found that they were hungry and sad. Joe suddenly felt the need to help them. As Joe continued walking, he came across a food truck that served pasta, soup and salad. The smell of the food started to make Joe's mouth water and he felt hungry. It reminded him of the homeless family, so when he went up to the truck to order some food, he asked to see the owner. As the man walked up to him, Joe looked into his emotions and found that the man loved to help charity and help the homeless.

The two talked for about thirty minutes, and he convinced the owner to go around the streets of downtown Seattle for the next three days, to give food to the homeless. The kind act resulted in many happy faces, and the food truck also received many more customers who were eager to hear more about it. Like this, Joe used his unique powers to help a great number of people do a number of things.

When he grew older, Joe started a company where people could donate money to help people in need, and Joe became a very well-known philanthropist. He dedicated his time and energy to make the world a better place for thousands of people around the world.

Joe exhibited personal power because although he could have used his powers for greed and just for himself, he used them for the good of the people. Joe was a person who always knew what the right thing to do was, and he did it well.

Self Esteem

Shaded Thoughts | Be friendly! Don't make assumption about people because the first interaction was not positive.

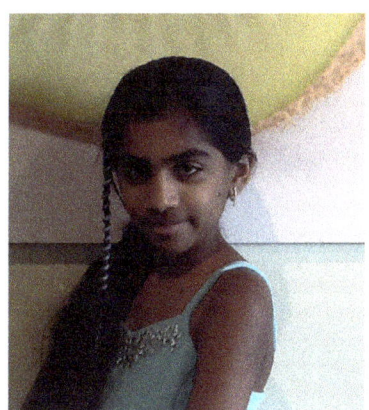

Vennela Panja

Vennela is in the fourth grade. She likes to help her community because it feels like she is helping herself! Her hobbies are anything artsy, swimming, biking, singing, and going outside.

Fiona was never what you would call a shy girl. She was energetic and passionate, and fully believed in her abilities. Thanks to her high opinion of herself, she had an air of confidence that made everyone like her. She knew that she was a fun person to be around, so she was always friendly and talkative with everyone that she met.

Entering her math classroom one day, Fiona saw a new student sitting next to her maple wood desk. She brightened instantly and went up to go say "Hi!"

To her surprise, the girl simply looked down and didn't say anything. After a few minutes of trying to initiate a conversation, Fiona realized that the girl simply wasn't going to respond. The bell soon rang, however, and Fiona was forced to end the attempt. Although she tried to focus on the teacher, Fiona couldn't help but wonder why the new girl didn't want to talk to her. Trying to subtly look behind her, Fiona noticed that it wasn't just her that the new girl was avoiding. The girl couldn't even look straight at the teacher without blushing and looking back down at the floor.

Fiona suddenly realized why the new girl wouldn't talk with her. She was just really shy! New found determination filled Fiona, and she decided that no matter what, she would become friends with this girl.

At the end of class, Fiona turned around to face the girl before they both left the class. "It was nice to meet you, although I didn't really get to know your name. See you again tomorrow." Hearing this, the girl's brown eyes moved slightly upward. "Alice." She whispered through half closed lips. Fiona beamed at hearing this and actually began to look forward to seeing Alice tomorrow.

Every day after that, Alice began to talk to Fiona a little bit more, and soon, was even talking to other people. Alice's self-esteem grew thanks to Fiona's kindness and friendliness, and she was happier than ever because now she knew that she was a great person who could be liked for who she was.

Sense of Purpose

An Encounter with Messi

If you lead your life with a sense of purpose, you can achieve great things.

Nicolas Miguel

Nico plays soccer and loves it with a passion. He is Argentinian and speaks Spanish fluently. He serves in a soup kitchen every week and enjoys public speaking but considers soccer his first love.

Sebastian was a soccer fanatic. His favorite team was the Barcelona Futbol Club (Barcelona FC). Unfortunately, Sebastian lived in a town where soccer wasn't really popular. Sebastian didn't like other sports like baseball or basketball, and no one else he knew liked to play soccer. Because of a lack of popularity for the sport, there weren't a lot of soccer fields in the town. This might have discouraged a lot of kids from playing soccer, but nothing could stop Sebastian from becoming a professional soccer player, which he felt was his dream and purpose in life.

Countless hours were spent on his driveway shooting at his garage, working on skill moves, and improving his speed. Sebastian became very good with his footwork, but couldn't show his skills to anyone because no one else plays soccer.

One day, Sebastian read in the newspaper that the Barcelona FC players were staying just outside the town and were doing a publicity event. Sebastian could barely contain his happiness, and had his father promise to take him to it.

As he waited in line to speak to the players, he thought about what he would say to these soccer legends. When he got to the front, Lionel Messi, one of the greatest soccer players in the world, smiled at him and asked him his name. Sebastian was speechless as he stared at his idol. He finally managed to introduce himself and said that he loved playing soccer, but was one of the only kids who played it in town. He also met the other players, people who he had only seen on television.

Near the end of the event, random kids were chosen to play a quick game of soccer with the team, and to Sebastian's surprise, he was chosen. Everyone was amazed at how good Sebastian was at soccer, and they found that he was a brilliant player and could one day be as good as the Barcelona players. The manager asked Sebastian if it was alright if they watched him play and helped to train him until he was old enough to join the team. Sebastian was thrilled and accepted. He had a sense of purpose, and because he never gave up, he achieved his goal in life.

Positive View of Personal Future

Dreams of a Better Future

Viewing your future in a positive way can empower you to become a better person.

Abi Opincarne and Katie Hansen

Abi and Katie are both in ninth grade. They love to draw and explore. Abi volunteers at various animal shelters during the summer. Abi is very passionate about singing and making everyone equal. Katie's very passionate about karate. She helps her community by teaching young kids how to defend themselves while teaching them life skills like respect, honestly, and other similar traits.

No one could say that Jennifer lived in a great neighborhood. She lived in an orphanage and didn't go to that good of a school. She couldn't read or write so well and wasn't very motivated to learn. Jennifer was pessimistic about her future, and didn't believe that she had a way to get a good job when she was older and didn't have many friends because of her negative attitude. She constantly thought about how little she would achieve in life.

One night, she had an incredible dream. In it, she imagined herself as a plant with another plant behind her as dark blue skies above her. The plant behind her began to grow into a much bigger plant, and wrapped itself around the plant she imagined herself as.

When she woke up, she realized that this represented her becoming and joining something greater and more powerful than herself. Jennifer was filled with an intense feeling of happiness. She felt that something very important was going to happen. She skipped across the orphanage while she did her chores. Then, to her delight, a couple came in who wanted to adopt a young girl. After looking around, they spotted Jennifer, and decided that she was the one she wanted to adopt. Jennifer felt that she could cry with happiness to finally be part of a family.

As she got to know her new family, she learned that they were great people, and immediately began to love them. She was enrolled in a great school, and had a tutor to help her catch up. Jennifer's full potential was realized, and she did great in school. She graduated from Harvard and started her own company, making millions of dollars. Her life was a great success because she changed her negative view on her future, into a positive one.

Mega Events Highlights

Wow! We were so inspired by the talented youth in our community! We celebrated this talent during the 40 Story's Mega Event. This was a huge celebration with performers, speakers, and awards.

The 40 Story's Mega Event was an event filled with many laughs, interesting story's, and fun experiences. We even unveiled the 40 Story's Leadership Book Cover to the audience. We had a number of inspirational speeches (some even by kids!), a thrilling award ceremony, Ya group macarena dance lead by YMCA, and a Bollywood routine by local dancers.

Here are a few highlights from the event:

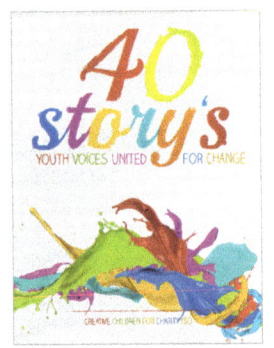

Unveiling of 40 Story's Leadership Book Cover

With the Help of Aktar Badshah, the Senior Director of Community Affairs at Microsoft we were able to unveil the 40 Story's Leadership book cover. Before we unveiled the book cover we asked our community to give us feedback. By having them vote on three different choices. There was an overwhelming vote on the current book cover design.

Art Display of 40 Leadership Assets

All of the 40 Paintings were showcased at the event. Each painting was beautifully framed with white mat and had beautiful titles. People spent lots of time admiring all the beautiful work.

Award Ceremony to recognize 55 youth leaders

We had 8 amazing community leaders who helped us to acknowledge the 55 youth leaders for all their hard work and dedication. Each participant received a trophy as well as a bag with lots of fun gifts.

Inspirational Speeches

We had many inspirational speeches from a number of youth leaders. They talked about a variety of topics, including Higher Expectations, Sense of Purpose, Empowerment from the perspective of youth, and Empowerment from the perspective of a parent. All of the speakers were amazing and inspiring.

Bollywood Performances

Local Bollywood dancers performed a traditional Indian dance routine to kick off our event. They were one of the many performances during our celebration. They performed a beautiful routine, wearing gorgeous dresses. You could hear the sequins on their skirts jingling as they danced. The music was enlightening; it was a sight to see.

SPECIAL THANK YOU FOR SUPPORTING THE "40 STORY" PROJECT

- Agustina Reishman
- Akhtar Badshah
- Amy Hansen
- Andrew and Sandy Tang
- Andrew Leubner
- Archana Sunil
- Barbara Rasmussen
- Barnali Dutta
- Billie Otto
- Bonnhi Chowdhury
- Brett Holmes
- Chaitra Vedullapalli
- Charlene Rouse
- Cindy Valdrez
- Claudia Sassano
- Davies Chirwa
- Dawn Sanders
- Debbie Pettersson
- Duane Draper
- Eric Bulley
- Erin Loman Jeck
- Gemma Edwards
- George Jennings
- Heather Matthews
- Heather Rasmussen
- Heidi Johnson
- Helena Valentin
- Hope Szudzik
- Isabel Bilotte
- Isabel Bilotte
- Janie and Brad Ojeda
- Jenny Kolln
- Jim Clark
- Joelle Skaga Nausin
- Joseph Bosch
- Judy Smith
- Julie Schuster
- Karen Abel
- Karen Sherman
- Karl Reese
- Kerstin O'Sheilds
- Lakshmi Sunku
- Linda Chandler
- Marcia Isenberger
- Marcie Maxwell
- Naveen Vig
- Neerja Joshi
- Neetha Tuluri
- Nickie Alexander
- Nicoleta Ispas
- Nikhil Kaza
- Pallavi Gajula
- Prasad Mettu
- Priya Talrej
- Rachel Cui
- Rachel Van Winkle
- Ram Dutt
- Ripal Shah
- Rodney Hines
- Sameera Goteti
- Sanjana Jain
- Shailaja Shetty
- Shirley Eclipse
- Shivaji Dutta
- Son Michael Pham
- Vijay Garg
- Vinay Kshirsagar

TO THOSE WHO MADE THIS BOOK POSSIBLE

- Albert Mensah
- Bryan Heathman
- Chaitra Vedullapalli
- DeeDee Heathman
- Kathy Knox
- Marian Peters
- Marty Evans
- Michael Tetteh
- Mike Peters
- Shiksha Arun
- Souptik De

TO THE INDIEGOGO SUPPORTERS WHO SUPPORTED US

- Agustina Reisman
- Alekhya Alavilli
- Alexis Gormley
- Amitabh Saran
- Anamika Malhotra
- Billie R Otto
- Bruce Gillespie
- Cathi Hatch
- Chaya Kamchetty
- Colleen M Gagley
- Conn A Standfield
- Dale L Rasmussen
- Dawn Sanders
- Deborah J Sogge
- Heather Matthews
- Hope Szudzik
- Howard Schaengold
- Isabel Bilotte
- Johan Valentin
- John and Amy L Hansen
- Judith L Kolln
- Julie Schuster
- Karl Franklin Reese
- Kartik Grover
- Linda J Chandler
- Michael Tetteh
- Naga Veni Mavuri
- Nakeesa M Frazier
- Pallavi Gajula
- Piya Haldar
- Prasad Mettu
- Rachel Mathison
- Rajesh Setty
- Robert A Bunge
- Robert S Ackerman
- Rohan Lam
- Samir Saluja
- Shanti Pattnaik
- Shirley Eclipse Chinery
- Shivaji Dutta
- Srinivas N Jay
- Tanaya Pattnaik
- Tejas Dixit
- Teresa R Teague-Vesey
- Ulhas Kotha
- Venkataraman J Chittoor
- Vijayagopal Thiruvengadam
- Vishwanathan Raman
- William Poole

www.ingramcontent.com/pod-product-compliance
Lightning Source LLC
LaVergne TN
LVHW072011060526
838200LV00010B/330